First World War
and Army of Occupation
War Diary
France, Belgium and Germany

5 DIVISION
Divisional Troops
205 Machine Gun Company
24 October 1916 - 30 November 1917

WO95/1539/2

The Naval & Military Press Ltd
www.nmarchive.com
Published in association with The National Archives

Published by

The Naval & Military Press Ltd

Unit 10 Ridgewood Industrial Park,

Uckfield, East Sussex,

TN22 5QE England

Tel: +44 (0) 1825 749494

www.naval-military-press.com

www.nmarchive.com

This diary has been reprinted in facsimile from the original. Any imperfections are inevitably reproduced and the quality may fall short of modern type and cartographic standards.

© **Crown Copyright**
Images reproduced by permission of The National Archives, London, England, 2015.

Contents

Document type	Place/Title	Date From	Date To
Heading	WO95/1539/2		
Heading	5th Division 205th M.G.A.C. 24th 10-16 To November 1917		
War Diary	Belton Park	24/10/1916	10/02/1917
War Diary	Grantham	10/02/1917	10/02/1917
War Diary	Elmstead Essex	10/02/1917	15/03/1917
War Diary	Southampton	15/03/1917	15/03/1917
War Diary	Havre	16/03/1917	18/03/1917
War Diary	Bethune	19/03/1917	20/03/1917
War Diary	Ferfay	20/03/1917	30/03/1917
Heading	205th Machine Gun Company 5th Division April 1917		
War Diary	Ferfay	01/04/1917	01/04/1917
War Diary	Chateau-De-La-Haie	01/04/1917	07/04/1917
War Diary	Canadian M G.C. Camp (XIA)	07/04/1917	12/04/1917
War Diary	Canadian M.G.C Camp	12/04/1917	19/04/1917
War Diary	Carency	20/04/1917	26/04/1917
War Diary	Canadian (XI) M.G.C Camp	27/04/1917	30/04/1917
War Diary	Canadian M.G.C Camp (X.I.A) (Map ref : France 36 B 1/40,000)	01/05/1917	04/05/1917
War Diary	Roclincourt (A28 B)	05/05/1917	10/05/1917
War Diary	Roclincourt Area	11/05/1917	15/05/1917
War Diary	Roclincourt Area (51 N B.W. Map Ref)	16/05/1917	23/05/1917
War Diary	Roclincourt Area	24/05/1917	25/05/1917
War Diary	Ourton	26/05/1917	15/06/1917
War Diary	In Action	16/06/1917	30/06/1917
War Diary	Roclincourt	01/07/1917	08/09/1917
War Diary	ACQ	09/09/1917	09/09/1917
War Diary	Liencourt	10/09/1917	10/09/1917
War Diary	Oppy	11/09/1917	25/09/1917
War Diary	Hellebrouck	26/09/1917	28/09/1917
War Diary	Wallon Cappel	29/09/1917	29/09/1917
War Diary	Berthen	30/09/1917	30/09/1917
War Diary	Berthen Area	01/10/1917	01/10/1917
War Diary	Dickebusch	02/10/1917	02/10/1917
War Diary	Ridge Wood	03/10/1917	12/10/1917
War Diary	Derby Camp G.32 D 3/2	13/10/1917	22/10/1917
War Diary	Westoutre Area G32 D 3/2	22/10/1917	24/10/1917
War Diary	Wiltshire Camp H 35C3/1	26/10/1917	31/10/1917
War Diary	Dickebusch Area Sheet 28	01/11/1917	06/11/1917
War Diary	Dickebusch Area	07/11/1917	10/11/1917
War Diary	Westoutre Area	11/11/1917	15/11/1917
War Diary	Lumbres Area Ref. Map	16/11/1917	16/11/1917
War Diary	Hazebrouck & Calais 13	17/11/1917	17/11/1917
War Diary	Combined	18/11/1917	23/11/1917
War Diary	Thiembonne Area	24/11/1917	24/11/1917
War Diary	St. Pol Area	25/11/1917	30/11/1917
Heading	War Diary 205th Machine Gun Coy. Dec 1-Dec 31st 1917		

WO 95/1539/2

5th Division
205th M.G.B.C.

24th 10-16. To ~~31st 12-17~~ NOVEMBER 1917

(ITALY)

Army Form C. 2118.

WAR DIARY
or
INTELLIGENCE SUMMARY.
(Erase heading not required.) No. 205 Company, Machine Gun Corps. Vol I

Instructions regarding War Diaries and Intelligence Summaries are contained in F. S. Regs., Part II. and the Staff Manual respectively. Title pages will be prepared in manuscript.

Place	Date	Hour	Summary of Events and Information	Remarks and references to Appendices
BELTON PARK GRANTHAM	24/10/16 to 5/2		Mobilizing and trained at BELTON PARK, GRANTHAM.	Queries
GRANTHAM	10/3/17	12.35 p.m.	Entrained for ELMSTEAD.	Queries
ELMSTEAD ESSEX	10/3/17 to 15/3/17	7pm	Detrained at WIVENHOE STATION and billeted in ELMSTEAD and attached to 198 Infantry Brigade, 66th Division.	Queries
"	15/3/17	3.25 am	Entrained at WIVENHOE STATION for SOUTHAMPTON - 3 R&File left behind.	Queries
SOUTHAMPTON	15/3/17	11 am	Detrained and proceeded to FRANCE.	Queries
"	15/3/17	5.30 pm	Sailed for FRANCE.	Queries
HAVRE	16/3/17	3 pm	Disembarked and proceeded to No 2 REST CAMP.	Queries
"	17/3/17	10 am	1 N.Co. admitted to hospital through disease leaving strength of Company 183 all ranks.	Queries
"	18/3/17	11 am	Received orders to leave No 2 Camp for entraining.	Queries
" to BETHUNE	18/3/17	9.30 pm	Entrained and proceeded to BETHUNE.	Queries
BETHUNE	19/3/17	6 pm	Detrained and billeted the Company in MONTMORENCY BARRACKS, and received orders to join 5th Division as Div: M.G. Company the next day. 2Lieut: H.C. OUGTON and 1 Private admitted to 18th Field Ambulance at BETHUNE with disease.	Queries
"	20/3/17	12 Noon	Proceeded by march route to FERFAY.	Queries
FERFAY	20/3/17	5 pm	Arrives at FERFAY and billets the Company.	Queries
"	25/3/17	5 pm	1 N.Co. admitted to hospital owing to injury.	Queries
"	23/3/17	4 pm	14 men 1/6 A & S Hrs, 5 men 1/8 Surrey Regt, 2 men 14/R War: Regt, 1 man 19/R War: Regt, transferred/joined	Queries

2353 Wt. W2544/1454 700,000 5/15 D. D. & L. A.D.S.S. Forms/C. 2118.

Army Form C. 2118.

WAR DIARY
or
INTELLIGENCE SUMMARY.   No 205 Company Machine Gun Corps
(Erase heading not required.)

Place	Date	Hour	Summary of Events and Information	Remarks and references to Appendices
FERFAY	23/3/17	4 p.m.	1 man 1/R.W. Kent Regt + 1 man 2/K.O.S.B. joined this Company as ammunition carriers.	Quick
"	25/3/17	5 p.m.	1 man 1/Norfolk Regt, 2 men 1/Bedford Regt, 1 man 1/Cheshire Regt + 1 man 16/R. War. Regt joined the Company as ammunition carriers - making a total of 32.	Quick
"	26/3/15	7.30 a.m.	32 ammunition carriers commenced training in Machine Gun work.	Quick
"	30/3/17	8.115 a.m.	Received orders for the Company to proceed to GOUY-SERVINS on 1st April.	Quick

205th MACHINE GUN COMPANY

5th DIVISION

APRIL 1917

Army Form C. 2118.

3052 M.T. Coy   Vol 2

WAR DIARY
or
INTELLIGENCE SUMMARY.
(Erase heading not required.)

Instructions regarding War Diaries and Intelligence Summaries are contained in F. S. Regs., Part II. and the Staff Manual respectively. Title pages will be prepared in manuscript.

Place	Date	Hour	Summary of Events and Information	Remarks and references to Appendices
FERFAY	1st/17	10 a.m.	Proceeded by march route to ST LAWRENCE CAMP CHATEAU-DE-LA-HAIE via HOUDAIN — GRAND SERVINS — GOUY SERVINS.	
CHATEAU DE LA HAIE	1st/17	4.15 p.m.	Arrived at CHATEAU DE LA HAIE and encamped at ST LAWRENCE Camp under canvas.	
"	1st/17	8 P.M.	Received orders for 1 section to go to the trenches in S.O.O. at 9.30 a.m. 2nd April 1917	
"	2nd/17	9 a.m.	No. 6 Section (2 officers + 31 O.R.) proceeded on foot to trenches of No. 11 Corp S.O.O. to furnish S.O.O. and carrying parties at night for nights 2/3 — 3/4 April	
"	3rd/17	4.10 p.m.	No. 2 Section (1 officer + 31 O.R.) proceeded to trenches S.O.O. and relieved No. 6 Section during nights of 3rd April — 4th April. No. 6 Section returned to Camp 3rd April.	
"	4th/17	7 a.m.	No. 3 Section (2 officers + 31 O.R.) relieved No. 2 Section in trenches at S.O.O. returning to Camp — No. 2 + 3 Section had some casualties. 1 killed 3 wounded. Aeroplane hovering over Camp dropping No. of bombs. No damage.	
"	5/17	4.15 a.m.	No 4 Section (2 offices + 31 O.R.) relieved No. 3 Section at S.O.O. — No. 3 Section returned to Camp.	

2353 Wt. W2544/1454 700,000 5/15 D. D. & L. A.D.S.S. Forms/C. 2118.

WAR DIARY
or
INTELLIGENCE SUMMARY.
(Erase heading not required.)

Army Form C. 2118.

Instructions regarding War Diaries and Intelligence Summaries are contained in F. S. Regs., Part II. and the Staff Manual respectively. Title pages will be prepared in manuscript.

Place	Date	Hour	Summary of Events and Information	Remarks and references to Appendices
CHATEAU-DE LA HAIE	5/17	4.15PM	5.00 April Individual fire [illegible] to #1 & #2 sections	
"	"	6.15PM	1 Officer & 144 O.R. proceed to find M.G. emplacements to the G.O.C sections of M.G. emplacements	
"	6/17	4 PM	4 men from the Company at [illegible] elements	
"	"	7.30PM	2 Officers & 65 O.R. proceed to S.P. 6 & 7 to unload 8 M.G. emplacements allot carriers 10,000 rounds ammunition to two posts & man the shelter trench in the front line [illegible] by regiments	
"	7/17	10.30AM	No 3 Section 2 officers & 108 O.R. left the Ch. de la Haie to [illegible] Camp at XIA	
"	"	11AM	New Company moved from ST LAWRENCE Camp to Ch. de la Haie Camp at XIA	
Canadian M.G.C. Camp XIA	"	2PM	Reg.No/9 Army/Vimy/36/06/M3	
"	"		All ops required for 2 Battns to occupy front line R13 & 90 +5 - S4a 02 20 am 8th April to positions commencing Zero 5.30 am 9th April also 15,000 rounds S.A.A to be taken [illegible]	
"	"	7.30AM	1 Officer & 60 OR proceeded to S13 & 90 +5 - S1 & 0234 NSLR 15 rounds	

2353 Wt. W2544/1454 700,000 5/15 D. D. & L. A.D.S.S.-Forms/C. 2118.

WAR DIARY or INTELLIGENCE SUMMARY

Army Form C. 2118.

(Erase heading not required.)

Place	Date	Hour	Summary of Events and Information	Remarks and references to Appendices
CANADIAN M.G. (Camp Hut)	7/4/17	7.30 pm	Ammunition & bombs and flares & rockets returned to Corps Dump.	
"	8/4/17		To Camp No. 1 Hut Section Camp.	
"		3 pm	No. 2 Section (1 Officer & 1 NCO) proceeds to position S13.6.90.45 & S14.0.23+ to operation on 9th April along the Q.6. Company and 15 BDE front to CABARET ROUGE (Rawlins's Advance S.D.) & establish Communication with position No. 2 & Battn.	
"		5pm	Staff received for Section to occupy Rawlins's S14.b.60.5. S14.a.5.80. on 9th April by 10 pm.	
"	8/4/17	4 pm	No. 1 & 4 Sections move from Verdrel S.11.c.6.5 track line S13.d.90.15 S14.a.023+ in operation commencing 9th April.	
"	9/4/17	5.30am	No. 2 & 4 Sections at S13 & 9045 to S14.a.023+ carried out operations of getting guns into the WOLF posns. for new front 30' Guns. 7.30 Lines of Battn. at Adv. D.D. - Mr. Caballero. 9 ammunition carriers carried up in reserve. Stupendous work in getting up and bringing in wounded under heavy shrapnel shells. Op. orders No. 2 & 4 Sections. The above (see App.) were.	

(CABARET-ROUGE & Regt. Hd. Qr. M.G.C. Camp Huts.)

WAR DIARY
INTELLIGENCE SUMMARY

Army Form C. 2118.

Place	Date	Hour	Summary of Events and Information	Remarks and references to Appendices
CANADIAN M.G. Camp (R)	9/7	7.30pm	No. 1 & 3 Sections proceeded to reinforce Sta 6160 & Sta 5580.	
"	"	7.40pm	Received a message that Yukon M.M.G. Battery wounded relief of No. 3 & Sections were to be in Camp Reserve	
"	"	7.50pm	Orders sent to Yukon M.M.G. Battery for Nos. 1 & 3 sections to return to Camp at 7/a. M. Relief by Yukon M.M.G. Battery Nos. 2 & 4 sections to Returned to Camp 7/a. 3.	
"	10/7	2am	Company in Camp at 7/a	
"	11/7	8pm	Company proceeded to positions in SOUCHEZ Switch Line. Nos. 2 & 4 Sections at Sta 8015 & No. 1 & 3 sections at Sta 7050 by reliefs Hd. Qrs. were at Sta 8015. Communication maintained between 1 & 3 sections & H.Q. by means of telephone & between D.M.G.O. CABARET ROUGE by means of runners.	
"	12/7	4.30am	Barrage fire at the rate of 10 rounds per gun per hour was given on the hour during attack on PIMPLE by the 10th CANAD. INF. BRIG & DG Weather at time of attack foul snow - rain fog - snow and intermittent blizzard being experienced. Blowing was not up at intervals.	

Army Form C. 2118.

WAR DIARY
or
INTELLIGENCE SUMMARY.

(Erase heading not required.)

Instructions regarding War Diaries and Intelligence Summaries are contained in F. S. Regs., Part II. and the Staff Manual respectively. Title pages will be prepared in manuscript.

Place	Date	Hour	Summary of Events and Information	Remarks and references to Appendices
CANADIAN M.G.C.Coys.	12/7/17	10 A.M.	Positions held intact by enemy airplane.	
"	"	7.30am	Position subject to attention from enemy artillery-Barrage	
"	13/7/17		Up to 4 a.m. shelling continues all night from situation purposes	
"	"	5.30am	No. 1 Section of works to No 2 CRATER (S.15.d.3.6.5) relief of Section of 16th Canadian M.G. Coy.	
"	"	6.30am	No. 2 & 3 Sections received orders to withdraw to Camp X.10.	
"	14/7/17	2.30am	No. 2 & 4 Sections at Camp X.10.	
"	"	7.17pm	Bde Hdqrs No 1 Section withdrew and No 1 Section relieved by Section of 15th Infantry Brigade No 1. Long Reservoir Trench	
"			Casualties: Nil	
"			Company in Reserve at X.10	
"	15/7/17		do	
"	16/7/17		do	
"	17/7/17		do	
"	18/7/17		do	
"	19/7/17	12am	2 & 4 Sections proceeded to No. 15 & 11.8.0.8.5 in the firing line. The Sections also placed in the reserve line Plate No. 2 & No. 3	

Army Form C. 2118.

WAR DIARY
or
INTELLIGENCE SUMMARY.
(Erase heading not required.)

Instructions regarding War Diaries and Intelligence Summaries are contained in F.S. Regs., Part II. and the Staff Manual respectively. Title pages will be prepared in manuscript.

Place	Date	Hour	Summary of Events and Information	Remarks and references to Appendices
CANADIAN M.R.R.Cam	1917	12 noon	The outpost system is occupied positions in S.S.A. in S.D.A. + S.D.A. + S.D.A. No 3 Platoon in S.S-A.	Weather – No 3 Platoon reports no enemy to report.
"		2 PM	H.Q. 4 gp training. 2 Cop moves to CAREAVY to relieve 2nd Lt. R.W. Bernstein reports pranks.	
CAREAVY	20/17		No 2 + 3 Platoons still in line – 1 + 4 Platoons in Camp (reserve).	
"	21/17		Lieut. L.J. McAVOY (2nd in Command) slightly wounded in foot (?) Shell fire while proceeding to line. 2nd Lieut. L.D. GLEDHILL assumes duties as 2nd in command. 1 O.R. wounded (remains on duty) + 3 Ridings O.Rs. wounded.	
			6m/ 64 ranges 2H gpts established at S+30 + 10.40	
"	22/17	2 pm	1 + 4 Platoons move 5 du rots in CAVALIER TUNNEL	
		5 pm	(8-10 30fs) in reserve. The EATON + BORDEN Canada M.M.R. Battery (east 6guns) were attached to the Company in supporting attack 13" infantry Brigade on German positions South of AVION. They occupied 4 gun positions (ready about 2nd in Russel System. Great difficulty was experienced	

WAR DIARY or INTELLIGENCE SUMMARY

Army Form C. 2118.

Place	Date	Hour	Summary of Events and Information	Remarks and references to Appendices
CARENCY	22/7	5 pm	On getting up S.A.A. O.C. reports ready to fire on targets allotted by 13th Infantry Brigade by midnight.	
"	23/7	4.45 am	Barrage fire maintained for 62 minutes on allotted targets. 1 O.R. No 2 Section (Carney) slightly wounded in hand by shrapnel. Ammunition expenditure — See attached form.	
			Section fire withheld on S.O.S. 13th Infy Brigade form a firing line but further fire withheld pr order to return to camp CARENCY at 3 pm.	
"	24/7	5.30	No 1 & 4 Sections Orders from 13 Infantry Brigade for Canadian M.M.G. Coys. to return to their Bivouac — Own two cars routed at 6.30 pm	
		8.15 am	No 3 Section relief complete	
		10 pm	No 2 Section do	
"	25/7		Lt. O.I.R. reports no reinforcements from ETAPLES. 2 men reported sick on returning from line. Company at CARENCY Camp.	
"	26/7		Company moves from CARENCY Camp to CANADIAN H.Q.C. Camp (H.Q.)	

Army Form C. 2118.

WAR DIARY
or
INTELLIGENCE SUMMARY.
(Erase heading not required.)

Instructions regarding War Diaries and Intelligence Summaries are contained in F. S. Regs., Part II. and the Staff Manual respectively. Title pages will be prepared in manuscript.

Place	Date	Hour	Summary of Events and Information	Remarks and references to Appendices
CANADIAN M.G.C. Camp	24/7		Company in training at X.1.a. 2 men report sick. 1 O.R. died of wounds.	
"	25/7		Company in training at X.1.a. 1 Rein. ottoman discharges to Fet. 1 man sent to No.2 C.C.S.	
"	29/7		2nd Lieut N.G. CARLAW joined the Company for duty. Company in training at X.1.a.	
"	30/7		do Church parade at 6 p.m.	

Army Form C. 2118.

205 Company M.G.C.

Vol 3

WAR DIARY
or
INTELLIGENCE SUMMARY
(Erase heading not required.)

Place	Date	Hour	Summary of Events and Information	Remarks and references to Appendices
CANADIAN M.G.C. CAMP (X.1.a.) Map ref: France 36B 1/40,000	1st/7/17		Company in Training at X.1.a.	App. 1
	2/7/17		Company in Training at X.1.a. 2 OR admitted to Field Ambulance - sick	App. 2
	3/7/17		Company in Training at X.1.a. Receives warning order to move to Roelincourt on ti/mor.	App. 3
	4/7/17		Move to be completed by 1 p.m.	App. 4
		8.30am	Company moves from M.G. Camp (X.1.a) to Roelincourt Area A. Transport lines at A.22 (Map Ref: 51.B.NW.France 1/20,000) and Company at A.28.6. in Bivouacs. Company to act in support respects to XIII Corps on relieving 2nd Division.	App. 5
Roelincourt (A.28.6.)	5/7/17		Company in Reserve at A.28.6.	App. 6
"	6/7/17		—do—	App. 7
"	7/7/17		Company in Reserve at A.28.6. Received wire to be ready that we are to come under orders of B.G.C. left Brigade right Division (13th Brigade 5th Division).	App. 8
"		9-15pm	Slight hostile shelling round our area (A.28.6.)	App. 9

Army Form C. 2118.

WAR DIARY
or
INTELLIGENCE SUMMARY
(Erase heading not required.)

205 Company M.G.C.

Place	Date	Hour	Summary of Events and Information	Remarks and references to Appendices
Roclincourt Area	8/5/17	11-20am	Received orders by wire from Company to move up to direct support to Major Cutting (D.M.G.O) at B.15 Central (Map 51B.N.W.) One officer to go up at once. No 1-2-3 rt Section in trench from B.11.d.40/70 to B.11.d.55/40 to give barrage fire indirectly on FRESNOY. for attack by 13th & 9th Infantry Brigades. Zero hour 5AM. This barrage was made to conform with artillery rifle & was maintained at 300 rpm in advance of artillery barrage. The following rifle & This barrage was belonging to 1st Machine Gun Inn Canadian Corps Squadron Regt 5th Can Division Captured the Bury 19th Bau Infantry Regt - 1st BATTALION 19th morning opposite FRESNOY - 1st BATTALION 19th Bavarian Regt suffers severe casualties from our M.G fire. Other Photos very heavily hit for Shell.	B.S.
	9/5/17		Barrages readjusted to deal with country between OPPY and FRESNOY No 3 Section relieves no Section 13th M. G. Coy in barrage position at B.11.c.10/50. No 2 Section withdrawn to Camp R.Q- INCOURT area in front & in rear of Section. S.A.A dumps & all back tracks heavily shelled. 2Lt HARRIS came up to Advance H.Q as 2/Command.	
	10/17			
	"	7.30pm	Very heavy bomb advancement by the enemy at 7.30 pm	Enf.

Army Form C. 2118.

WAR DIARY
or
INTELLIGENCE SUMMARY

(Erase heading not required.)

205 Company M.G.C.

Place	Date	Hour	Summary of Events and Information	Remarks and references to Appendices
Roclincourt AREA	11/5/17		No. 1 Section positions shelled more heavily than usual. No further Casualties but no damage reported. Heavy bombardment by our artillery at 7.30 pm. 1 O.R. wounded through hand. 1 O.R. killed. Received orders from advanced H.Q. to 1 Officer + 1 O.R. to report there B.15 Central (Map Ref: 51B N.W.)	25 g
"	9/5/17		2 Officers from Base + 1 O.R. Join Company for duty.	25 g
"	10/5/17		2 O.R. Slightly wounded but remain at duty. LENS–ARRAS (Roclincourt AREA) Subject to hostile artillery fire between 4-5pm. 1 officer wounded.	25 g
"	12/5/17	6.30 am	Heavy bombardment by our artillery. Officer went into the trenches 5. 13th M.G. Coys on account of shortage of their officers. Orders received for relief of No. + Section by No. 3 Section on the night of 13th inst. 1 O.R. wounded.	25 g
	13/5/17		No. 3 Section + 1 Officer relieves No. + Section in No. + Section as usual. 1 officer is kept at Adv. H.Q. (B.15 Central) 25 g	25 g
	14/5/17		Situation as usual. 1 officer is kept at Adv. H.Q. (B.15 Central) 25 g	25 g
	15/5/17	3 pm	Received order from A.H.Q that No + Section at Base (A + B 3) to relieve No 1 +# Section on night of the 16th inst.	25 g

WAR DIARY
or
INTELLIGENCE SUMMARY

205-Company M.G.C

Army Form C. 2118.

Place	Date	Hour	Summary of Events and Information	Remarks and references to Appendices
ROULINCOURT AREA. (5TH B.N)	16/5/17		4 O.R. joined Company as reinforcements. No 4 Section relieves No 1 Section in No 1 Coy position (B11640/70-58 11&50/40)	
	17/5/17		1 Officer returns to Camp. Situation quiet.	
	18/5/17		1 O.R. killed in action & 3 O.R. wounded during bombardment on night of 17/18th inst. Date on night of 18th 1 O.R. killed.	
	19/5/17		No 1 Section relieves No 3 Section in No 3 Coy position. No 3 withdraws to ROCLINCOURT.	
	20/5/17		Situation Normal. No 4 Section moves & goes to New position in No 1 Group	
	21/5/17		Situation quiet.	
	21/5/17		1 O.R. sent to Corps Rest Camp - Boulogne. Received orders to relief of 5th Division by 2nd Division.	
	22/5/17 12 Midnight		No 4 Section relieved by 1st Cavalry Division. Coy Advances to ROCLINCOURT Relief Completes 2nd M.G. Squadron returns to Q (A.25.b.6).	
	23/5/17		Nothing of importance	

Army Form C. 2118.

WAR DIARY
or
INTELLIGENCE SUMMARY

(Erase heading not required.)

205 Company M. G. C.

Instructions regarding War Diaries and Intelligence Summaries are contained in F. S. Regs., Part II. and the Staff Manual respectively. Title Pages will be prepared in manuscript.

Place	Date	Hour	Summary of Events and Information	Remarks and references to Appendices
ROCLINCOURT AREA	24/7	12 mid night	No 1 & 2 Sections on 5th Division relief relief was others to withdraw to ROCLINCOURT.	J.R.G.
"	"	9 AM	2 officers & 90 O.R. proceed to advance party's scene this	J.R.G.
"	25-5	3 PM	at OURTON. (Mid Rd. end. 11)	J.R.G.
"	"	6.30 PM	Company moves by bus to OURTON vis BRUAY	J.R.G.
"	"		Company arrives at OURTON.	J.R.G.
OURTON	26/7		In training at OURTON.	J.R.G.
"	27/7		" "	J.R.G.
"	28/7		" "	J.R.G.
"	29/7		3. O.R. Two Company as reinforcements. In training at OURTON	J.R.G.
"	30/7		In training at OURTON	J.R.G.
"	31/7		do	J.R.G.

Army Form C. 2118.

WAR DIARY
or
INTELLIGENCE SUMMARY
(Erase heading not required.)

205TH Machine Gun Company.   Vol 4

Place	Date	Hour	Summary of Events and Information	Remarks and references to Appendices
OURTON	1/7/19		In training at OURTON 1 OR joined as reinforcement 1 Officer started for leave to UK	
do	2/6/19		In training at OURTON 1 O.R. returned from Field Ambulance	
do	3/6/19		Company attended Church Parade	
do	4/6/19		Company in training 1 OR returned from Field Ambulance	
do	5/6/19		Company in training 1 Corporal joined as reinforcement, 2 O.R.s returned from Base Hospital, 1 OR left for UK Army of occupation West Europe	
do	6/6/19		Company in training 1 OR returns from 1 st Army West Europe	
do	7/6/19		Company in training	
do	8/6/19		Company in training	
do	9/6/19		Company in training	

WAR DIARY or INTELLIGENCE SUMMARY

Army Form C. 2118.

205th (Machine Gun) Coy

Place	Date	Hour	Summary of Events and Information	Remarks and references to Appendices
OURTON	10/6/17		Company attended Church Parade	
do	11/6/17		Company in training	
do	12/6/17		Company in training	
do	13/6/17		Company in training	
do	14/6/17		Received orders at 4pm for Coy to proceed to A27.d.7.7. ECURIE (Ref map 51 B N.W.) on the 15th inst. Orders received at midnight 13/6/17 that one section was to relieve positions 17.d.20 (174 M.G. Coy Trench mortars). No 3 section proceeded by bus with guns and all trench kit on morning of 14th & occupied positions.	
do	15/6/17		Company move by bus to A27 d.7.7. (ECURIE 1st map 51 B N.W.) ECURIE Camp. Transport lines at new positions at A27 d.9.6. No 1 section & No 6 section proceeded line at 8pm, positions 1st 5 occupied (ref map Gun positions GAVRELLE & 17.d.20 occupied	
Sin Station	16/6/17		Everything very quiet. No casualties	

WAR DIARY or INTELLIGENCE SUMMARY

Army Form C. 2118.

205th Machine Gun Coy

(Erase heading not required.)

Instructions regarding War Diaries and Intelligence Summaries are contained in F. S. Regs., Part II. and the Staff Manual respectively. Title Pages will be prepared in manuscript.

Place	Date	Hour	Summary of Events and Information	Remarks and references to Appendices
In action	17/6/17		Everything very quiet. No casualties. 1 Officer left for leave to UK	
do	18/6/17		Situation normal in all positions. Divisional Sports held. Company stove 3 row props in Machine Gun Coy turnouts (limited)(Comments)	
do	19/6/17		No 2 Section relieved No 3 Section on the night 19/20th. 1 OR left for front stunt Rest Camp	
do	20/6/17		Situation Quiet. 250 Rounds used by No 4 Section on this deranged work	
do	21/6/17		Situation Normal	
do	22/6/17		Situation unchanged	
do	23/6/17		Situation Normal, 1 Officer slightly wounded by shrapnel & afterwards discharged by an Officer of the A.V.C. 1 O.R. joined as reinforcement. During the day orders were received to prepare 16 positions for guns to give barrage fire for the attack on Oppy trench by 13th Inf Bgde	
do	24/6/17		Situation Quiet. Reaching topless & work on them commenced	
do	25/6/17		Work on Emplacement continued, clearance Headquarters established	

Army Form C. 2118.

WAR DIARY
or
INTELLIGENCE SUMMARY

(Erase heading not required.) 203rd Machine Gun Coy

Instructions regarding War Diaries and Intelligence Summaries are contained in F. S. Regs., Part II. and the Staff Manual respectively. Title Pages will be prepared in manuscript.

Place	Date	Hour	Summary of Events and Information	Remarks and references to Appendices
In station	26/6/17		Situation Quiet. Work on emplacements continued. S.A.A. dumped near them.	
	27/6/17		No 3 Section proceeded to the line to take over new positions from in the Corps Line relieved by those of the 13th Company, relief completed at 4.20 a.m. Work on new positions complete & new positions occupied a further 60,000 rounds S.A.A. taken up. Positions etc as under.	

Barrage No	No of Guns	No of Section	Position of Section	Targets
1	4	2	B.11.a.3.9.	Area bounded by lines from G.13.c.2.5. to G.13.c.4.0. to G.13.a.0.7. to G.13.a.2.5. to G.13.c.2.5.
2	4	1	B.11.a.5.25.	do
6	4	4	B.11.a.9.5.	Area bounded by lines from G.13.a.2.5. to G.13.a.0.4. to G.7.c.6.1.6. to G.13.a.2.5.
7	4	3	B.11.b.1.5.	Area bounded by lines from G.1.c.7.5. to G.1.c.5.7. to G.25.d.7.4. to G.1.a.5.6. to G.1.c.7.5.

Army Form C. 2118.

WAR DIARY
or
INTELLIGENCE SUMMARY

(Erase heading not required.)

205th Machine Gun Company

Place	Date	Hour	Summary of Events and Information	Remarks and references to Appendices
En Action	28/6/17		Zero Hour 7.10 pm	
			Rates of fire allotted as follows	
			Zero + 1 minute to Zero + 40 minutes 1 belt per gun per 5 minutes	
			Zero + 40 " to 5 am 29 minute 2 belts per gun per hour	
			In event of an S.O.S. rapid fire to be given	
			About 8.30 pm One Gun & Tripod dislodged by shell fire also 3 O.P's	
			of W.O.4 helio wounded.	
			Enemy Barrage slow in starting	
			Enemy Barrage ceased about 9.45 pm but several shells till 1 am 29 inst afterwards quiet.	
			Enemy operations a heavy thunderstorm Guns were going well & providing little retaliation except between 8.15 & 9 pm when O.P. 4 Helton were heavily shelled.	
			Fire maintained by all except damaged guns	
			At 9.30 pm what appeared to be meant for an S.O.S. signal was put up top out troops near South edge of OPPY WOOD Rapid fire was at once opened and excellent work done by two men an example of extreme coolness under heavy shell fire which kept on most noticeable effect.	
			At the time the S.O.S. went up the Artillery were quick & returning seventeen were very thickes with the Barrage people they fancied	

Army Form C. 2118.

WAR DIARY
or
INTELLIGENCE SUMMARY

(*Erase heading not required.*) O 205th Machine Gun Coy

Place	Date	Hour	Summary of Events and Information	Remarks and references to Appendices
In action	29/6/17		Situation Normal. Sectors in same position. Sending MGs for S.O.S. Ammunition with Sectors made up to 20,000 rounds per Sector. Copy of Complimentary report received from General Officer Commanding 13th Bde. "My best thanks for all the assistance you gave to the Brigade under my Command in our very successful attack yesterday"	
do	30/6/17		Situation Normal. Sectors all OK	

[signature] CAPT. COMMANDING
205TH COY. M.G.C.

Army Form C. 2118.

WAR DIARY
or
INTELLIGENCE SUMMARY

(Erase heading not required.)

205th Machine Gun Coy

Instructions regarding War Diaries and Intelligence Summaries are contained in F. S. Regs., Part II. and the Staff Manual respectively. Title Pages will be prepared in manuscript.

Place	Date	Hour	Summary of Events and Information	Remarks and references to Appendices
RECLINCOURT	1/7/17		3 Sections in the line. 1 Harassing section goes up at dark. Harassed Sgt Bristow's Barrage point.	
	2/7/17		No 2 Section relieved & presumed 7500 of line 13 ex day. Situation Quiet.	
	3/7/17		Situation Quiet except till about 12.35 p.m. when enemy put up a heavy barrage on the ANZLEUX LOOP & paid attention to back areas. 1 Man hurt by pom. Received opr by Y.E. Hill. Capt Tyrrell 7.5 company proceeded on leave to U.K.	
	4/7/17		No 2 Section fired 12 KLS on enemy working party. Situation abnormal.	
	5/7/17		On duty of 96. 182th Sections returned to Camp (ECURIE WOOD HUTS) there was Gun 2 teams of No 1 Enemy during the night in gaps in enemy wire worked to keep them down. 4 belts using 12 mins between the hours of 10.30 p.m. & 1.30 a.m. S.A.A. expenses 2020 Rounds.	
	6/7/17		On the night of the 6/7th No 1 Section were relieved by the 159th M.G. Coy Guns during the night on enemy wire ammunition expended 3500 rounds	

Army Form C. 2118.

WAR DIARY
or
INTELLIGENCE SUMMARY
(Erase heading not required.)

205th M. Gun Coy.

Place	Date	Hour	Summary of Events and Information	Remarks and references to Appendices
ROCLINCOURT	7/7/17	—	Situation Quiet	
	8/7/17	—	Situation Normal. Men not in trenches attended Church parade.	
	9/7/17		Captain W.O.B. Herbert went to camp vacated by Barnsley Pioneers Shape went in front of ELLIS & WOOD. Transport lines did not move. Preliminary orders received for machine gun co-operation on raid on FRESNOY TRENCH between T30 d 95/20 & T30 d 5/4 (Ref map GAVRELLE 1-10,000). 24 machine guns were to be employed in this operation divided into 3 groups. No. 1 Group, the Company supplying about 3 Groups each group consisting of four guns. Sites recommended + positions for approaches traverse as follows. No. 1 Group at B 11.5 5/6 & 5 3 Groups at T 29 & 9/5.	
	10/7/17		Situation Normal. One man wounded on sentry hours of the night by shell but evacuated after bit. Pairs distributed by field love Party the night much was engaged or new positions for the Work.	
	11/7/17		3 O.R. temporary left on the night 11/12 W.O.2 section relieved NO 3 in the line. Situation Normal. Work continued during the night on new positions.	
	12/7/17		Situation Quiet. Visit from Divisional conference. 7th Group moved for this Company transferred to 215th Divisional Employment Coy.	

2449 Wt. W14957/Mgo 750,000 1/16 J.B.C. & A. Forms/C.2118/12.

Army Form C. 2118.

WAR DIARY
or
INTELLIGENCE SUMMARY
(Erase heading not required.)

205th M. Gun Coy

Place	Date	Hour	Summary of Events and Information	Remarks and references to Appendices
ROCLINCOURT	13/4/17		No 1 Section proceed to line & take up positions for No 1 Barrage	
			No 3 Barrage	
			In order to give Barrage fire for the space our FRESNOY TRENCH by our Barren East barrage sgl. Target all no counter	
				REF MAP GAYRELLE 1/20,000
			Group No.	Rate of fire
			No 1 Section Positions B.11.d.5/6	Targets &c.
				Be points the right flank of the Raid
			No 3 Group T.29 & 0/5	from zero to zero+45" One bell your guns per minute
				Two guns to capture French from 61a.1/3 to 61a.4/6 One guns to Barrage French from 61a.4/6 to 61a.25/80
				from zero to zero+45" To barrage along a line from T.35 a.9/0 to a.25 a.25/15	One belt per guns per four minutes
				ZERO HOUR 3 AM	

WAR DIARY
or
INTELLIGENCE SUMMARY
(Erase heading not required.)

Army Form C. 2118.

705th M. Siege Bty.

Place	Date	Hour	Summary of Events and Information	Remarks and references to Appendices
ROCLINCOURT	13/7/17		All guns in position. During the day 11.15 pm Weather very unsettled + very heavy rain. The Depot was in direction of the last moment by these groups fired some 19,000 rounds S.A.A. Fired.	
	16/7/17		Having early morning 4/4/17 8.30 4 Lieuten returned to Corps HQ. Returning on the evening Lieuten Simmons.	
	17/7/17		Lieuten Kemp & Cooper Ripre returned from leave to U.K.	
	18/7/17		Lieuten Simmons, Greves were stationed in the evening that the Most would come off on the morning of the 19th inst. & that we would occupy positions for Nos 1 + 3 groups & also were the left four guns of No 2 group. Its 2 groups as shewn on preliminary order targets & as follows. No 1 Group of 8 guns at U.35 c 53/20 and U.35 d 44/14 to provide Barrage on front of reading country from zero to zero +6 to Barrage along line from U.25 a 55/40 to U.25 a 2/1. Zero +6 zero +.45 to Barrage along a line from U.25 a 5/6 to U.25 a 5/2	
	19/7/17		Lieutens go up to see to occupy position for Barrage Zero during Raid. Captn Wyatt goes up to advanced Headquarters Marchwiel. Me 2.40 Colo leaves for Rest Camp + Pte Bradshaw proceeds to London Course	

WAR DIARY or INTELLIGENCE SUMMARY

Army Form C. 2118.

205th M. Gun Coy.

Place	Date	Hour	Summary of Events and Information	Remarks and references to Appendices
ROCLINCOURT	9/4/17	3.30 a.m.	Zero hour on 9th. + all guns opened fire in time allotted 15 mts after Zero H.M. Later airs had guns en action on ENEMY TRENCH and heavily shelled. This shelling was continuous + several enemy were seen to fall near the parallax. One of the emplacements received a direct hit + put gun stopped spare parts. Enemy gun crew. Casualties were totally destroyed two gun numbers 66335 pte Fitzpatrick + 66555 pte Hampton were killed outside + the remainder of the team wounded. The rest of the teams were very busy shooting at short task. Gun Sergt F14115, + got the Snipers 253595 wounded. Shortly after this the guns ceased firing + Shortly after that the gun was shifted to emplacement S 67845 though emplacements enemy + continued. Afterwards continued with their good shooting on enemy + their infantry that were seen retiring to freeze successfully. Also operations to shift his own enemy tank happened. The M.G.O at once began its way to the 'Y' any of the two new into actual + shortly knew to advance, were advised until the guns etc. After digging wound on permanent cover for some time. They found that it was no avail + set shelter to dug for the guns etc. But after the operation was over + received cover himself in the remainder of the section returned to their billets to their new H.Q.O. mortally escorted The Lewis officer 2/Lt Hambr to get the men off safely to their billets after very heavy + persistent shell fire. This M.G.O. has been commended its military skill for his great courage + devotion. Pte Parker Lewis Officer again showed great coolness + his attack gallantry assisted on the engagement. Rounds fired 27,250.	

Army Form C. 2118.

WAR DIARY
or
INTELLIGENCE SUMMARY
(Erase heading not required.)

6. 205th M. Gun Coy.

Place	Date	Hour	Summary of Events and Information	Remarks and references to Appendices
ROLLINCOURT	19/7/19		No 3 Section made a good deal of attention & were steadily shelled the whole time; the general round their being heavily torn up but the section escaped all serious inj- -uries, unsupported from 5 minutes after Zero onwards. 6.57.A1. Test firing & own wounded on Lens Lys.	
	19/7/19		Sections dispositions as follows:— No 1 guns at K.6.d. 40/90, B.4.B.25/30, B.5.w 34/35, B.5.w 15/90, No 3 Section B.11.a 75/30, B.11.a 70/35, B.5.d 2.90/0, B.5.c 45/45. No 2 Section as coy & also as positions in Lens Line. Upon typed letters up Section of D.M.G.O. no places of Major watching and issued to NK No OS Hempo taking over.	
	20/7/19		Situation unchanged — work continued in corps line.	
	21/7/19		Situation quiet — Capt Croft Caputer goes to 3rd Army Signal School for course.	
	22/7/19		Situation Quiet.	
	23/7/19		2nd Lt Tempany & Sgt. No 2 Section relieved No 1 Section. A2EL Force.	
	24/7/19		Night firing on Bovres trenches at C.7.A.1/1. & tejtory of lights Railway on rear Ronda force 3600.	

WAR DIARY
or
INTELLIGENCE SUMMARY

(Erase heading not required.)

205th M. Gun Coy

Army Form C. 2118.

Place	Date	Hour	Summary of Events and Information	Remarks and references to Appendices
ROCLINCOURT	25/7/17		Expedition Party of Brigade relieved 2/1 Thanks on the line P56 Brocklehurst returns from Lantern Course.	
	26/7/17		Erection of dugouts. New emplacements sites + work commenced.	
	27/7/17		Dewey & Lytell + 26,27 men + Barracy O.C. was discharged on the following area in the Brigade line FRESNOY TRENCH returned first stage + Gypsy support trench also in FRESNOY village & W.P.O. 3 guns of tho temporary co-operation try gun on new ground behind on line from U25 a 20/15 & U25 c 33/30 barrage particulars of FRESNOY ALLEY from U25 c 35/60 to U25 c 90/85 rates of fire as follows 3min +1 a 3ms +7. 1 rifle per gun
			$\quad$ 3ms +7, +30. $\quad$ 1 rifle to 5 minutes
			$\quad$ 3ms +61, +80. $\quad$ 2 rifles to 8 minutes
			Total rounds fired 7500 Rounds	
	28/7/17		No. 1 section proceed to Camp to relieve No 4 section No 4 to Camp 2/1 Thanks leave for course at CAMIERS 4th & S.M. Simmonds in charge to O.M. Work in new emplacements continued	

Army Form C. 2118.

WAR DIARY
or
INTELLIGENCE SUMMARY
(Erase heading not required.)

(8) 205th M. Gun Coy.

Place	Date	Hour.	Summary of Events and Information	Remarks and references to Appendices
ROCLINCOURT	29/7/17		Situation Quiet. One of Gunners wounded. W.D.S. Stopped airplane crash on rest positions returned	
	30/7/17		Situation Normal. Neglect fired on CRUCIFIX LANE rounds fired 2750	
	31/7/17		Situation Normal. Night firing on Cross Roads at 67 d 04/13 Rounds used 2500	

[signature] CAPT. COMMANDING
205TH COY. M.G.C.

Army Form C. 2118.

WAR DIARY
or
INTELLIGENCE SUMMARY

(Erase heading not required.)

235 M.G. Coy. M   6

Place	Date	Hour	Summary of Events and Information	Remarks and references to Appendices
ROCLINCOURT	1/9/17		3 Section in the line. Remaining Section Battalion Camp. Situation normal. Enemy 3.5"/11" explosive Jew carried out on Gun Rear Jet C7 d 84/75. 20000 rounds fired.	
	2/9/17		No. 4 Section relief No. 3 Section in RED LINE. No. 3 Section return to camp. 3 O.R. arrived to F.A.	
	3/9/17		Right of Sec. very Carriers out on Batt. Hot Pro at C.130.90.70. Slow fires going on very exp. 2/3" Some stood over to late enemy going. Carriers carried out on new shoot.	8000 yd. range
	4/9/17		Situation normal. Reg. to being carried out on Reserve Enemy Hyde Redoubt. Enemy carried out on Battn. offensive Loop at C7c 15/45.	
	5/9/17		Enemy Camels Gun in camp. 4 Hotts machine Gun at C7c 15/45. Enemy machine Gun silenced. Hostile machine gun at C7c 15/45"	
	6/9/17		Going Carrier out on bank every 12.30 m. About 1.45 a.m. heavy enemy Barrage put down on our front & support lines. Enemy strafed trenches ARLEUX LOOP. Barrage SOS sent in from OPPY on our SOS Stand to in reply. Enemy Barrage Bn opened & died down continued.	

2449 Wt. W14957/M90 750,000 1/16 J.R.C. & A. Forms/C.2118/12.

Army Form C. 2118.

WAR DIARY
or
INTELLIGENCE SUMMARY

(Erase heading not required.)

205- M.G. Coy.

Instructions regarding War Diaries and Intelligence Summaries are contained in F.S. Regs., Part II. and the Staff Manual respectively. Title Pages will be prepared in manuscript.

Place	Date	Hour	Summary of Events and Information	Remarks and references to Appendices
ROELINCOURT	7/9/17		Night firing on guns at C76 00/25. Ammun. expended 3000 rds. Work on gun positions & S.A.A. dump for new position No. 3 Section phoned to him to relieve No. 2 Section. No 2 Section relieved. Sent Capt. Hyde forward to arrange for advance Coy. H.Q. & gladiolis station to camp. 2nd Warner arrived on leave to 16. 4 (8 to 6 10 o'c). 1 O.R. evacuated to C.C.S.	
	8/9/17		Night firing on track & railway crossing at C76 00/25. Ammun. expended 1500 rounds.	
	9/9/17		Situation normal. 3000 rounds fired on Cross Track fired by enemy.	
	10/9/17		Situation normal. 3000 rounds fired on enemy track firing out C1 d 35/40. (1000 yds) Right firing carried out on Batln. Hd. Qs. at C13 a 97/0. Enemy Held up heavy barrage on Right section at 12 midnight. Our S.O.S. also was fired. Did not reply to Jerry Sector too.	
	11/9/17		Situation quiet. During night "11/12 enemy heavy artillery attention to Kaien areas. Jerry upset. Mainly by shelling near Bangalore. Coy. Ready to man all of our Guns: Seld in reserve. No. 3 section relieved No. 1 Section in the line. Night firing carried out on enemy Cross Track at C7 a 7/25. Ammun. expended 3000 rounds.	
	12/9/17		Track firing at C1 a 73/25 shelled heavily from 3000 rounds.	
	13/9/17		Ammunition expended 3000 rounds. Enemy gun team clear for reply of enemy. No shoots to 7 Brigade moved to ANZIN	

Army Form C. 2118.

WAR DIARY
or
INTELLIGENCE SUMMARY

(Erase heading not required.)

26.5- N.G. Coy

Place	Date	Hour	Summary of Events and Information	Remarks and references to Appendices
RECLINGHEM	14/9/17		Situation quiet. Byte firing on enemy at C7a 0/25. 2500 rounds fired.	
	15/9/17		Situation normal. Byte firing carried out on enemy by harassing fire. Trench elem U26.02.14/4/4 + C1a 38/44. Ammun expended 3000.	
	16/9/17		Situation enemy quiet. Byte firing on new work carried out at C7a 97/46 - C7a 97/49. Ammun expended 3000 rounds.	
	17/9/17		No.6 Section return to camp on relief by No.1 section. Cpl. Edwards + No.1 Ration convoys by machine gun fire brought onto cross roads at C7 & 25/00. No.1 Ration convoys of Tilques ~ Railway crossing + going fed. Byte firing on bytes at C, at 50/00. Ammunition gun works. Gates + Jacques (Gulsko) at C7 a 81/60. + C7 a 81/77. Ammunition 3000 rounds on each.	
	18/9/17		Situation normal. Ammunition expended 1500. Lewis constructed at C7 + C6.94/3.	
	19/9/17		Byte firing on Cross Roads at C7 a 81/77. Ammun expended 900 rounds. On night 19/20-th E Special Coy R.E.'s engaged and the operation, but the operations were delayed to enemy offence the 7.30 t. at 1.30. In conjunction with operation ammun expended 13,750 rounds. Enemy return fire as under.	

No. of Gun	Target		Time	Rate of fire
	From	To		
8	U.25 c 0/0	T.30 d 9/2	Zero plus 5 minutes to Zero plus 4 hours.	Zero + 5 min. to Zero + 25 min. 1 belt per 5 min.
9	T.30 d 9/2	T.30 d 55/45		
14	U.25 c 55/40	U.25 c 32/81		Zero + 25 min. to Zero + 4 hours Burst of 30 rounds each 5 min.
17	U.25 c 58/40	U.25 c 30/81		
19	U.25 a 3/0	U.25 a 25/15		
15	U.25 a 25/15	U.25 a 15/35		

2449 Wt. W14957/M90 750,000 1/16 J.B.C. & A. Forms/C.2118/12.

WAR DIARY or INTELLIGENCE SUMMARY

Army Form C. 2118.

205 M.G. Coy

Place	Date	Hour	Summary of Events and Information	Remarks and references to Appendices
ROCLINCOURT	20/8/17		Belt firing during the night 19/20th on New work under construction at OC7a 89/80 + OC7a 89/77. Barbed wire on work there.	
	21/8/17		4000 rounds expended on work there.	
	22/8/17		No. 4 Section proceeded to line to relieve No. 3 Section. No. 2 Section in CORPS LINE. No. 3 section return to camp. Night firing on Gun Track at C7.c.14/30 + C7a 87/23. 3000 rounds.	
	23/8/17		Situation normal. Indirect fire carried out on dumps at C7.c.09/30 + C7.b. Junction of tracks at C1.c. 50/80. 3000 rounds spent.	
	24/8/17		Retaliation quiet. 3000 rounds fired on Track at C1.d. 50/80. + also on Junction of Enemy Narrow Gau at C7c 15/45. + also on strong point + light firing on Dump opposite 3000 rounds. At C1a 57/81. Down Cross Track at C7.c.15/50 + also on Salient exchange. 1500 rounds fired on C7c 50/0.	
	25/8/17		Batts. Hd. Qrs. at C7c 50/0.	
	26/8/17		Night firing on Dumps at C7.b 07/03. Dumps opposite 3000yds. Situation normal.	
	27/8/17		3000 rds fired on New Work under construction at C7 a 97/1. R.E.s + C7a 94/59. 1 Section of 90 Rounds by 5 offcrs by 3 guns on each of M.G.25.c 47.91 + M.G.25.c 30.17 [illegible] between M.G.25.c 47.91 + M.G.25.c 30.17 Motor & M.G.25.d 45/45 - M.G.25.c 47/91. Also on M.G.25.c 35/75. M.G on M.G.25/d 45/45. Aimed at M.G.25.c 30/75 - M.G.25.a 27/35. camellas M.G.25 + 30/75. M.G.25.a 27/35. + M.G.25.a 20/70. M.G.25.a 27/35.

Army Form C. 2118.

WAR DIARY
or
INTELLIGENCE SUMMARY

(Erase heading not required.)

30o- M.G. Coy

Instructions regarding War Diaries and Intelligence Summaries are contained in F. S. Regs., Part II. and the Staff Manual respectively. Title Pages will be prepared in manuscript.

Place	Date	Hour	Summary of Events and Information	Remarks and references to Appendices
ROCLINCOURT	29/9/17		Relieved Normal. On night 29/30 E Special Coy R.E's dropped gas bombs on enemy trench system from T.39.c to T.30.c. 61 Battalion very keen to observe this, Coy. fires 10,000 rounds in conjunction with the barrage as under:—	
			No. of Gun / Target — From / To / Time	
			16 M.25.c 25/45 M.25.c 45/45 Zero + 5 min to End of firing	
			17 M.25.c 45/75 M.25.c 35/75 Zero + 15 min to "	1 Belt per L. gun
			8 M.25.c 35/75 M.25.c 35/90 Zero + 15 min to "	
			10 M.25.c 35/90 M.25.a 25/05 Zero + 25 min to "	
			9 M.25.a 25/05 M.25.a 25/20 Zero + 30 min to "	
			19 M.25.a 25/20 M.25.a 25/35 Zero + 35 min to "	50 rounds per 10 gun
				Zero + 5 L.	
	30/9/17		Nothing firing on C.7. d 8.9.0. Barrage expended 3000 rounds.	
	3/10/17		Relieved unchanged. Relieved & discharged 3000 rds from 2 Guns of Track at C.1.d.5.9.0 & C.a.7.3/20.	

A. Shank pn.
CAPT. COMMANDING
205TH COY. M.G.C.

Army Form C. 2118.

205- M.G. Coy

WAR DIARY
or
INTELLIGENCE SUMMARY.
(Erase heading not required.)

Instructions regarding War Diaries and Intelligence Summaries are contained in F. S. Regs., Part II. and the Staff Manual respectively. Title pages will be prepared in manuscript.

Place	Date	Hour	Summary of Events and Information	Remarks and references to Appendices
ROCLINCOURT	1/9/17		Three sections in the line – 1 Section took of Cont. Front. Situation normal. Night firing at C.26 c.65.35 – New Switch Trench construction FRESNOY PARK & Commn. Effected Boropaume.	
	2/9/17		Situation quiet. 3000 Rds fired on Dump at C7.c.20/30 – & Trench & R.W. Crossing at C.1.6.65.90	
	3/9/17		Night firing on New Switch in FRESNOY PARK at C.28 c.54/63 Ammn. Expended 3000 rds.	
	4/9/17		Situation normal. Night firing on New Switch Trench at C.10.c 40/70. Ammn Expended 3000 rds. to C.8.a 45/44	
	5/9/17		200 rds fired on Concrete. Night firing on C.9.a. 97/66 & C.9.a 97/59 OPPY-NEUVIREUL ROAD C.3.6.62/90 C.3.c 25/20 C.3.c.36.10/30. C.14.a 17/70. Ammn. Expended 3000 rds.	
	6/9/17		Situation normal. 100 rds fire at Aircraft. 700 rds fired on factory Roof & Cross Track. { C.13.c. 65/35 – C.8.a 65/50 – C.13.c. 25/90 – C.13.8 29/10 Dump C.13.a 94/70 – Batn Hd. Qu. C.10.c 9½ – 9 ½ 50 – New Tunnel	
	7/9/17		Company relieved on the line by 92 M.G.Coy 31st Div. Transport lines & Coy. Farm at ECURIE. Relieved by 243rd M.G. Coy. 31st Div	

(A7094). Wt. W12839/M1293. 750,000. 1/17. D. D. & L. Ltd. Forms/C2118 T4

WAR DIARY or INTELLIGENCE SUMMARY

Army Form C. 2118.

205 M.G. Coy

Place	Date	Hour	Summary of Events and Information	Remarks and references to Appendices
ROCLINCOURT	9/9/17		Company moved at 10.15 am. Route to Junction of MAROEUIL & ECURIE Rds. 95th Bgd BM. to Joins. Rd to ACQ. passing N of CHASIRE BROCMOUT Rds & Ry Crossing at L.6.99/975 & Cross Rd at F.1.59.91. ECOIVRES - ACQ. Ry Stn at B.N.W. 5½ C.N.E. Coy billets in ACQ for one night.	
ACQ	9/9/17		Coy moved from ACQ to LIENCOURT (under canvas) 7 day rest regime in tents.	
LIENCOURT	12/9/17		Coy moved from LIENCOURT to OPPY to commence tour of 15 day Bgd Front. Arrived at OPPY 11.45 am. 1 officer 2nd Lt J.C. Butler + 4 OR's ret. sick from ex. 3rd Bgd	
OPPY	13/9/17		In trenches at OPPY. 2 officers & 14 OR's rejoined by D.M.S.C. Capt W.D.B. Reynolds from Regts leave U.K.	
	13/9/17		Coy in trenches. Lieut S.S. Harris time for ENGLAND having been granted indulgence M.G.O.T. Sch. 2nd Lieut A.J. SHANTH to be retained 2m on Commn Capt Hodder	
	13/9/17		Coy in trenches	
	14/9/17		Coy in trenches	

Army Form C. 2118.

WAR DIARY
or
INTELLIGENCE SUMMARY.
(Erase heading not required.)

205th M.G. Coy

Place	Date	Hour	Summary of Events and Information	Remarks and references to Appendices
OPPY	15/9/17		Coy in training. Lecture by D.M.G.O. on new Lewis Gun tactics &c.	
	16/9/17		Coy in training. Church parade for all Denominations.	
	17/9/17		Coy in training	
	18/9/17		Tactical Exercise on OPPY DISTRICT	
	19/9/17		Coy in training	
	20/9/17		Coy in training	
	21/9/17		Coy in training	
	22/9/17		Coy in training	
	23/9/17		Church parade.	
	24/9/17		Coy in training.	

Instructions regarding War Diaries and Intelligence Summaries are contained in F. S. Regs., Part II. and the Staff Manual respectively. Title pages will be prepared in manuscript.

Army Form C. 2118.

WAR DIARY
or
INTELLIGENCE SUMMARY.
(Erase heading not required.)

No 5 - M.G. Coy

Instructions regarding War Diaries and Intelligence Summaries are contained in F.S. Regs., Part II. and the Staff Manual respectively. Title pages will be prepared in manuscript.

Place	Date	Hour	Summary of Events and Information	Remarks and references to Appendices
OPPY	26/9/17		Division transferred from XIII Corps 1st Army to XIX Corps 5th Army. Entrained for ST. OMER. Entrained at 3 p.m. Detrained at ST. OMER at 10.30 p.m. Coy. move by march route to billets at HELLEBROUCK.	REF. MAP HELLEBROUCK. SHEET 5 A — No —
HELLEBROUCK	26/9/17		Coy. in training at HELLEBROUCK.	
	27/9/17		Coy. in training at HELLEBROUCK.	
	28/9/17		Coy. move by march route to WALLON CAPPEL via TILQUES and ARQUES. Coy. commenced at 9 a.m. Coy. arrive in billets at 7.30 p.m.	REF. MAP BELGIUM AND FRANCE SHEET 27
WALLON CAPPEL	29/9/17		Coy. move by march route to BERTHEN area. Coy. move at 8.45 a.m. — arrive in billets at R.36 or 3/4 R.36 or 3/4 at 10 a.m.	
BERTHEN	30/9/17		Church parade in the morning, received warning order for Coy. to proceed to forward area. Division on arrival in X corps area is transferred to X Corps from XIX Corps & from 5th Army to 2nd Army.	

A. Shank 2/Lt
for CAPT. COMMANDING
205TH COY. M.G.C.

Army Form C. 2118.

WAR DIARY
or
INTELLIGENCE SUMMARY.
(Erase heading not required.)

205 M.G. Coy.

Place	Date	Hour	Summary of Events and Information	Remarks and references to Appendices
BERTHEN AREA	1/10/17		Coy. proceeded by road & rail from R 26 d 3/4 (Ref Sht Sheet 28) to N° Central (Ref: Sht Sheet 28) (Belgium) France Area.	Ref: Trench Map Belgium France Sht 28
DICKEBUSCH	2/10/17		Fine reconnoitred & arrange positions. Coy moved from A.B.C. positions as follows:- B Battery J.14 d 9/5 (1) 3 Guns B Battery J.15 c 1/9 (6) B Battery C B Battery attacked - Both 2nd L Bastard commenced No.1 Guns commenced 2nd Lt Bostock " No 2 " " (8) Capt Wyatt attached No 2 L M.G. Coy) B & C Batteries A Battery (2 guns of 13 L M.G. Coy) at 12 midnight No C Gun Section commenced digging position to take charge of N.G. Section proceeded to Huts Aven move to 2nd Lt Wright Hd. Qrs at FITZCLARENCE FARM J14 d 9/5 Rear (Hd Qrs)	Ref Map Belgium Sheet 28 1/20,000
RIDGE WOOD	3/10/17		Hd. Qrs at RIDGE WOOD N5a 8/4. 4.30am. 3000.w. S.A.A. brought up to Section complete position by 5 am. D.A.A. At 6am each gun position Heavy Shelling during all day. Casualties each gun position process who kept Walker - L/Sgt Major For Top J.19.a. Capt Hyde Hd. Qrs Coy Hd Qrs at 13 L D.I. Brig. Hd. Qrs Lieut Walsh No 1. Stock Hut 9.0. Below in action at 10 p.m. L/C/Sgt Smyth " " " (The Glencoe below loose Hut in charge of a convoy J/19/c & Jim Transport.) lost in charge of S.A.A. & The (Wolvergheim) company of Bug Heavy Guns gun equipment & S.A.A. Enemy barrage	

Army Form C. 2118.

WAR DIARY
or
INTELLIGENCE SUMMARY.
(Erase heading not required)

205 - V.G. Coy

Place	Date	Hour	Summary of Events and Information	Remarks and references to Appendices
RIDGE WOOD	3/1/17		The Machine Guns of the YPRES-MENIN ROAD fired during the night a few short bursts harassing enemy communication from its battle positions — also a Vickers 7000 rounds S.A.A. per gun fired.	
	4/1/17		Zero hour for the attack of the 3rd Div on enemy front 6 a.m. 5 a.m. Batteries ready for action. 6.3 a.m. Barrage opened. Guns & Co. opened rapid harassing fire. 6.7.30 a.m. Battery fire at 6.35 — at 60 rounds per gun. Steady fire from 6.3 a.m. to 7.30 a.m. Battery fire from 12 noon to 1 p.m. — — 6.3 a.m. to 7.30 a.m. SOS all night. 7.30 a.m. Battery ceased fire — laws on SOS lines. Counter attack SOS signals from 6.8 am to 9.30 am and C Battery opened on SOS lines to C & B Battery. Very ? ? B Battery presence to Germans on (Retreat) from in front to pieces ? Gun there and of a dense ? from cloudy day — gun shoots rendered a dense fog in the evening. Square 30.11 Barrage fire. 2nd Lt. Brigham returned to unit. SOS 5000 SK — took over same — Slightly wounded for the moment & duty Hr. No ? during the day our action was ? Casualties 1 OR. (Refd Hotes) killed, 9 wounded. Enemy shelling very severe.	

Army Form C. 2118.

WAR DIARY
or
INTELLIGENCE SUMMARY.
(Erase heading not required.)

205 - M.G. Coy.

Instructions regarding War Diaries and Intelligence Summaries are contained in F.S. Regs., Part II. and the Staff Manual respectively. Title pages will be prepared in manuscript.

Place	Date	Hour	Summary of Events and Information	Remarks and references to Appendices
RIDGE WOOD	5/9/17		Situation good. No enemy during night 4/5-th. 4.30 to 6 am Enemy barrage very heavy. The gun crew of Stuart's hit. Captain gun lifted from gun emplacement & a new position taken from. The gunfire improved greatly, was changed into action again. SAA brought up to position during the early morning. 4000 S.A.A. per Battery given on S.O.S. Completely destroyed Ohio for on Battery gun pit. No.3 Section (Return to Camp) Regt returned by Lieut of 15-M.G. Coy. Brown 3.00 p.m. - B.T.C. Battery Brown [& a A & B] Battery could bring Comp. Capt Hyde Tolel casualties to date 2 killed, 15 wounded. 13 horses. 4 Guns out of action (changed).	Sgt Scott Killed 5/9/17 [?] 1/3 [?]
	6/9/17		No.3 Section arrived in camp at RIDGE WOOD at 6.8 am. Intricate... Went from Barrage Line changed at 4 am to another J17c 3½ to J17a 65¾0. Serving Hight & Two Churing Battery SOS signals their High Team were fired. SOS in a Battery Barrage then observed fire 5.5 pm to position near Cascade Farm = at Enemy Fught off & during and	
	7/9/17		Heavy shelling at intervals. SOS signals at 11.30 am from Ypres Common offensive opened from Battery 2½-3 [?] firing effective to camp. Casualties for the day 3 killed. 2 wounded 1 horse	
	8/9/17		No.5 Section under 2/Lt Bythin moved to line & relieve No.4 Section No.143 Section relieved by 13th M.G. Coy. No.1.2.7. Sections return to camp. Carrington Lavender	

(A7092). Wt. W12839/M1293. 750,000. 1/17. D. D. & L., Ltd. Forms/C.2118/14.

Army Form C. 2118.

WAR DIARY
or
INTELLIGENCE SUMMARY.
(Erase heading not required.)

205 - M.G. Coy

Place	Date	Hour	Summary of Events and Information	Remarks and references to Appendices
RIDGE WOOD	9/9/17		Capt Hyde return to Camp at 9 am. Maj Curtis M.C. (DMG) took over command of Group. Night party pushed to extreme, covered No. Bank. Clear over top to No. 3 section above by 1st & 2nd Bdges. I moved to carry the night Barrage 1 magazine.	
	10/9/17		No. 3 Section subjects to heavy shelling during the attack. Enemy opened 11,000 pdr.	
	11/9/17		Coy (less No. 3 Section) on the morning moved from WESTOUTRE AREA arriving in Camp at DERBY CAMP 5 30 am 3/2. No. 3 Section came under orders of B.S.C. 95th Inf Bn. No. 3 Section orders to withdraw for 2 hrs during relief manoeuvre 2nd Bde. Taking over 3 Coys in reserve. No. 3 Section took up position at RIDGE WOOD CAMP during the night in ZILLEBEKE.	
	12/9/17		No. 3 Section arrive in Camp at 5 30 at 1/2 at 2 km Capt. 95 Inf new notes to Commence of 13th M.G. Coy in command of Section MC (DM) at the 2 05 9/17 Maj. K.H. Curtis MC (DM) hands to command Capt. Cine O. Cook from 13th Coy to No. 3 Coy officer 19 ors. Coy on temporary from relieving M.Gun Field Coy to 12/9/13.	Cy. Ord. 9/9/17

Army Form C. 2118.

WAR DIARY
or
INTELLIGENCE SUMMARY.

(Erase heading not required.)

205- M.G. Coy

Place	Date	Hour	Summary of Events and Information	Remarks and references to Appendices
DERBY CAMP 53.a.3/2	23/10/17		Coy on training	Ref. Post Sheet 28
	14/9/17		Church Parade	
	15/9/17		Coy in training 10 ors join as reinforcements	
	16/9/17		Coy in training	
	17/9/17		Coy in training	
	18/9/17		Coy in training	
	19/9/17		Coy in training	
	20/9/17		Coy in training	
	21/9/17		Church Parade	
	22/9/17		Coy in training Coy Capt 2th Lieuts & 3 guns Adv. cav. at 8 pm to proceed to RIDGE WOOD pergments to reconneting its time on 23/9/17	Staff 25 V5 combat

WAR DIARY
or
INTELLIGENCE SUMMARY.
(Erase heading not required.)

205 - M.G. Coy.

Place	Date	Hour	Summary of Events and Information	Remarks and references to Appendices
WESTOUTRE AREA B.30.d.3/2	22/9/17	7.30 pm	Coy. proceeded by motor buses to RIDGE WOOD AREA & accommodated in tents & bivouacs at N.5.c.3/5. Reconnoitring party returned from line at 7.30 pm.	Reserve
	23/9/17		No. 1 & 2 Sections proceeded to line at 2.30 am to take up Barrage positions. Two Section of 13th & 15th Coys 10 OR of No. 4 taken & put to line to act as carrying party. Pilot parties to No. 1 & 2 Section guides at 4.17 am to lay T barrage colours. 2nd Guns arrived at Barrage Colours at 9.15 am No. 3 Section arrived from occupy Barrage position as Flashes/Nurses & ready to take up Con Cy of the Div at STIRLING CASTLE DUMP. Capt. Cook proceed to line at 4.30 am & took up his Pm at TOR TOP JUGS. 13th & 15th M.G. 4th Pm at chg of M.G. Support company & Batteries. Capt. Cook now in chg of A Battery and Battery Commander. No. 3 Section attached to 13th M.G. Coy. Capt. WAREHAM 2nd i/c. No. 1 & 2 Sections now known as B Battery B Battery Command 300 yards attack to B Battery Coy. HQrs Pm moved to WILTSHIRE CAMP at H.35.c.3/1. Casualties in the line for 24th NIL.	11.0 am GHELUVELT
	24/9/17		No. 3 Section heavily shelled getting gun at to front B Back area Enemy very quiet from 9.30 to 1 am	

Army Form C. 2118.

Army Form C. 2118.

WAR DIARY
or
INTELLIGENCE SUMMARY.
(Erase heading not required.)

205- M.G. Coy.

Place	Date	Hour	Summary of Events and Information	Remarks and references to Appendices
WILTSHIRE CAMP H.35.c.9.1	26/11/17		Zero hour for the attack by 5th Inf Bde on POLDERHOEK CHATEAU 3. 40am. A Battery of Vickers very lightly observed very well cover for the attack. 1 Gun complete also opened overhead barrage covering on team. All Guns carried out programme. Willis 4 wounded having Lewis cover. The Battery was B Battery were ordered to position to push all Guns in also heavy shelled. 3 OR's wounded. Action General 2 OR's wounded. Zero 6 Guns +170 Battery fired a creeping barrage for moving of 3 OR's wounded. A.C.E. 3. Co. B Battery Vickers on SOS lines - limbers at 8.30 attack. B Battery fired on SOS [?] Zero [?]. Hour were reported 11.30am. SOS was on our front line reported 11.30 - 11.30 our own troops were reported on to be [?] front line 12.30pm. 20 ten at 11.30 [?] off at times, all our [?] were got up, also a great deal of ammunition. B Battery was [?] rations 17 Barrage. The [?] of the Battery [?] here [?] [?] while the [?] The [?] [?] thanks. Sergeant [?] [?] Battalion on attaining his ranks of [?] [?] Class on being a [?] manner to send new [?] Vickers Gun to action Between [?] [?] [?] [?] [?] [?] [?] Chateau. Lieut [?] in Vickers on scored [?] [?] [?] [?] [?] Battery on [?] [?] Battery [?] [?] [?] [?] [?] [?] Battery C.G.	Sheet 28

Army Form C. 2118.

WAR DIARY
or
INTELLIGENCE SUMMARY
(*Erase heading not required.*)

205-M.G. Coy

Instructions regarding War Diaries and Intelligence Summaries are contained in F.S. Regs., Part II. and the Staff Manual respectively. Title Pages will be prepared in manuscript.

Place	Date	Hour	Summary of Events and Information	Remarks and references to Appendices
WILTSHIRE CAMP H.35.c.3/1.	26/9/17		A. managed 15 fires at the guns of this Battery on return. 5.20 pm S.O.S. again sighted — J Battery opened fire. Two Pks 2nd Batt. R.I. Rifles volunteered to carry-up ammunition to forward gun 13st M.G. Coy. 5.30 pm No. (3 Lewis) detachment posted in A Battery + return to camp. A.A. expended 40,000.	
	27/9/17		Situation quiet. M.M. awarded to L/Cpl Ayres (acc. + in A) Gdn. + Pte. Davidson for gallantry on 24/9/17. Baker + Pte. Rees very heavy.	
	28/9/17		Situation normal. Enemy shelled for ith very heavy.	
	29/9/17		No. 3 + 4 Teams relieve No. 1 + 2 teams in line at 6 am. Casualties during relief 5 wounded. Situation normal. Fog obscuring fire on STIRLING CASTLE. Dump taken 11.30 AM + 12.30 pm.	
	30/9/17		Enemy Coy H² Op'n again shelled wood gas shell. Casualties to No. 4 Section (B Battery) 1 killed 3 wounded.	
	31/10/17		During night 30/31st Rel'n No. 9.30 pm + 3 am. RIDGE WOOD + DICKEBOSCH Shelled by hostile aircraft 2 or more from line slightly gassed.	

G. Shanks M.
CAPT. COMMANDING
205 L.G. COY. M.G.C.

Army Form C. 2118.

WAR DIARY
or
INTELLIGENCE SUMMARY.
(Erase heading not required.)

205th M. Gun Company

Instructions regarding War Diaries and Intelligence Summaries are contained in F.S. Regs., Part II. and the Staff Manual respectively. Title pages will be prepared in manuscript.

Place	Date	Hour	Summary of Events and Information	Remarks and references to Appendices
DICKEBUSCH AREA	1/7	6am	2 sections in the line & 2 at rest. Captain Junction. Sterling Castle area subjected to gas shells. Casualties nil. 1 Officer & 2 O.R's from a reinforcement.	
SHEET 28.	2/7		Situation fairly quiet, 2 O.R's wounded "Gas". 2nd Lt. C.G. Carleos returns from leave to U.K.	
"	3/7		Situation quiet, 1 Casualties nil, 1 O.R. admitted to hospital. Wounded "Gas".	
"	4/7		Situation normal. Casualties, 1 O.R. wounded. 11 O.R. join as reinforcements.	
"	5/7	5am	1 Off., 3 N.C.O's & 21 men proceed to line to occupy positions at FITZCLARENCE FARM. Heavy enemy barrage placed on back areas. Casualties, 1 O.R. killed, 6 O.R. wounded. 1 Mule killed, 3 mules wounded. 5 O.R's join as reinforcements.	
"	6/7	6am	Position heavily barraged with the following casualties: 5 killed, 1 Died of Wounds, 4 wounded. 2 Ammo & Limbers destroyed by shell fire. 1000 rounds fired on CHATEAU POLDERHOEK.	

WAR DIARY or INTELLIGENCE SUMMARY

Place	Date	Hour	Summary of Events and Information	Remarks and references to Appendices
DICKEBUSCH AREA	7/7	7am	Situation fairly quiet. Casualties nil. OC Coy & 4 OR's return from Adv. Stnl. Coy to Rear Head Quarters at WILTSHIRE FARM, H.35.c.3/4 (ay map sheet 20).	
"	8/7		Situation normal. Casualties nil. 2 OR's join as reinforcements. Ridge Wood Dickebusch area heavily bombed by enemy aircraft from midnight to 4.30 am.	
"	9/7	4am	1 Officer, 3 NCO's + 30 men proceed to recce positions opposite Poelderhoek Chateau & 1 Officer, 3 NCO's & 32 men return to Rest Stn. Bn. Camp at WILTSHIRE FM. B Battery's S.O.S. switched on to J.16.a.90/70 & J.17.a.00/70. A Battery's S.O.S. switched on to J.17.a.00/20 & J.17.a.00/70. 3 O.R's join as reinforcements.	
"	10/7		Situation normal. Casualties nil. Received warning order for Coy to move to WESTOUTRE AREA on 11/7.	

Army Form C. 2118.

WAR DIARY
or
INTELLIGENCE SUMMARY.
(Erase heading not required.)

Instructions regarding War Diaries and Intelligence Summaries are contained in F. S. Regs., Part II. and the Staff Manual respectively. Title pages will be prepared in manuscript.

Place	Date	Hour	Summary of Events and Information	Remarks and references to Appendices
WESTOUTRE AREA	11/7	9am	Company (less 2 sections in the line) move by march route to Westoutre (WINCHESTER CAMP) M.16 a 6/4.	
		9-30	2 sections in the line on relief embus at SHRAPNEL CORNER & rejoin company at WINCHESTER CAMP. 3 OR's gun as reinforcement.	
	12/7		In training at WINCHESTER CAMP, WESTOUTRE. 25 OR's join as reinforcements. 1 OR dies of wounds + 1 OR evacuated to CCS sick.	
	13/7		In training at WINCHESTER CAMP, WESTOUTRE. 8 OR's evacuated to CCS sick.	
	14/7		In training at WINCHESTER CAMP, WESTOUTRE. 3 OR's evacuated to C.C.S. sick.	
	15/7		In training at WINCHESTER CAMP, WESTOUTRE. 2 Officers, 39 OR's & limbers proceed by march route to new area (LUMBRES). 1 Officer, 13 OR's entrain at OUDERDOM as advanced party to NEW AREA. 3 OR's evacuated to C.C.S. sick.	

WAR DIARY
or
INTELLIGENCE SUMMARY.

(Erase heading not required.)

Army Form C.2118.

Place	Date	Hour	Summary of Events and Information	Remarks and references to Appendices
LUMBRES AREA REF. MAP HAZEBROUCK & CALAIS 13 combined	16/7/17		Company move by march route to OUDERDOM to entrain for NEW AREA, LUMBRES.	
	17/7/17		In training at VAL-DE-LUMBRES. One Officer & 2 ORs proceed on leave to U.K.	
	18/7/17		In training at VAL-DE-LUMBRES.	
	19/7/17		1 OR joins as reinforcement, 1 OR evacuated to COS sick & 2 ORs detained at hospital sick.	
	20/7/17		In training at VAL-DE-LUMBRES. 1 OR admitted to Hosp sick.	
	21/7/17		In training at VAL-DE-LUMBRES. do	
			1 OR evacuated to C.C.S. sick	
	22/7/17		3 ORs admitted to Hosp. sick.	
			In training at VAL. DE LUMBRES. 2 ORs join as reinforcements.	
	23/7/17		2nd in Command reports from leave.	
			In training at VAL. DE. LUMBRES.	
			Coy received warning order to move under orders of 15th Inf. Bde.	

Army Form C. 2118.

WAR DIARY
or
INTELLIGENCE SUMMARY.

(Erase heading not required.)

Instructions regarding War Diaries and Intelligence Summaries are contained in F. S. Regs., Part II. and the Staff Manual respectively. Title pages will be prepared in manuscript.

Place	Date	Hour	Summary of Events and Information	Remarks and references to Appendices
THIEMBONNE AREA	24th	10 AM	Company moves by march route to MERCK ST LIEVIN & billets for one night.	
ST. POL AREA	25th	—	Coy. moves by march route to PREDEFIN & are billeted in the Chateau.	
	26th	—	Coy. in training at PREDEFIN.	
	27th	—		
	28th	—		
	29th	—		
	30th	2.30 pm	Coy. moves by march route to HESDIN to entrain for Italy. Entrainment complete by 11.30 pm.	

[signature]
CAPT. COMMANDING
205TH COY. M.G.C.

War Diary.

905th Machine Gun Coy.

Dec 1 - Dec 31st 1917.